JUST GRADUATED
Guided Journal

Preparing For Life After College

Created By **Sara Elizabeth Boehm**

Part Of The Essential Moving Guide Series

Copyright © 2016 by Sara Elizabeth Boehm

All rights reserved. No part of this publication may be reproduced, stored in a retrieval system, or transmitted in any form or by any means—electronic, mechanical, photocopy, recording or any other—except for brief quotations in printed reviews, without the prior permission of the author.

Cover Design: Ashley Boehm

First Edition

Available for bulk purchases in the U.S. by corporations, institutions, and other organizations. For more information, please contact our Customer Support Department at support@myessentialguide.com

Introduction

───────────────

Section One: *Graduation*

───────────────

Section Two: *Moving Forward & Settling In*

Introduction

Pomp and Circumstance Marches, caps and gowns, celebration, and nostalgia—that's right, it's graduation time. What lies in your future? You're likely heading toward a season of a lot of "firsts" or at least quite a few new beginnings.

As you look forward to the next chapter in your life, you may be feeling many things: excitement, anticipation, sadness, nervousness, or impatience. There are things that you can do and consider that may help ease your upcoming transition and make the most of your next few years. But it is up to you: to process, to explore, to take chances, and to make your new life what you want it to be!

Whether your next step is more school, a new job, travel, or exploration, you can use the prompts in this journal as a general guide to help you write about your experiences, feelings, and future plans. If you come to a question that you don't want to write about, cross it out and create your own. Journal here or use these prompts to fill your own online journal or blog. The format doesn't matter; simply do what best fits your style.

Congratulations, Graduate, your future awaits you!

~Graduation~

"Dear Past,

Thank you for the lessons.

Dear Future,

I am ready."

– Unknown

Graduation date:

_____

My college/university:

_____

City:

_____

My major(s):

_____

Where I am moving after graduation:

_____

_____

_____

When I think about graduating, the first word that comes to mind is _____ because:

_____

_____

_____

_____

_____

_____

_____

"It is what it is, but it will become what you make it." – Unknown

Where I see myself in 5 years:

_____

_____

_____

_____

_____

_____

_____

_____

_____

What small steps are you taking right now to set yourself on the right path toward this future?

_____

_____

_____

_____

_____

_____

_____

"Great people do things before they're ready. They do things before they know they can do it. Doing what you're afraid of, getting out of your comfort zone, taking risks like that—that's what life is. You might be really good. You might find out something about yourself that's really special and if you're not good, who cares? You tried something. Now you know something about yourself." – Amy Poehler

Thinking ahead to the upcoming year, I am most excited about . . .

"I believe that you are only in control of so much. So whatever you are not in control of you can't worry about." – Elizabeth Olsen

The most challenging aspect of the upcoming year will be . . .

"What comes easy won't last long. What lasts long won't come easy."
– Unknown

The things I will miss most about college are . . .

"Don't give up. Normally it is the last key on the ring which opens the door." – Paulo Coelho

The things I will miss least about college are . . .

"Embrace uncertainty. Some of the most beautiful chapters in our lives won't have a title until much later." – Bob Goff

Where are your friends headed after graduation?

Do you know anyone currently living in or moving to your destination city?

"Happiness is not something ready made. It comes from your own actions." – Dalai Lama XIV

I feel lucky that . . .

"Expect less, prepare more. Judge less, respect more. Take less, give more. Complain less, appreciate more." – Anonymous

Describe a few of your favorite college memories . . .

"We don't remember days, we remember moments." – Cesare Pavese

Looking back on your first months of college, how did you adjust and make friends? What would you do again? What would you do differently?

"When you focus on problems, you'll have more problems. When you focus on possibilities, you'll have more opportunities." – Unknown

What is it about you that makes you a good friend?

_____

_____

_____

_____

How would your friends describe you?

_____

_____

_____

_____

What do you look for in a close friend?

_____

_____

_____

_____

_____

_____

_____

"People inspire you, or they drain you. Pick them wisely."
– Hans F. Hansen

Looking forward, what makes you nervous? Can you address any of these concerns by talking to others?

"Be strong enough to stand alone, smart enough to know when you need help, and brave enough to ask for it." – Unknown

What are key items on your To-Do list right now?

_____
_____
_____
_____
_____
_____
_____
_____
_____

What is one thing you can do today to have a better tomorrow?

_____
_____
_____
_____
_____
_____
_____
_____
_____

"Energy is contagious, positive and negative alike. I will forever be mindful of what and who I am allowing in my space." – Alex Elle

Moving is a fresh start—in what way will you make this move a fresh start for you? *(Try out a new hobby, sport, or style. Resolve to address an issue you've been putting off. Make a New Year's-style resolution to become the best that you can be!)*

"If you don't like something, change it; if you can't change it, change the way you think about it." – Mary Engelbreit

3 things that I am grateful for are . . .

Take a few minutes each day to appreciate what is going well, no matter how small. It could be your health, a friend's or stranger's smile, a safe place to live, your pet, a book you are reading, or an event you enjoyed attending. Make it a daily habit!

Have you found a place (home, apt, condo) to live yet? How did you find it (or what are you looking for in your current search)?

_____
_____
_____
_____
_____
_____
_____
_____
_____
_____
_____
_____
_____
_____
_____
_____
_____
_____
_____

"If you're interested, you'll do what's convenient; if you're committed, you'll do whatever it takes." – John Assaraf

What was your favorite memory from the past week?

"I've learned that people will forget what you said, people will forget what you did, but people will never forget how you made them feel."
– Maya Angelou

Notes/Thoughts:

~Moving Forward, Settling In~

"The best advice I've ever received is, 'No one else knows what they're doing either.' "

– Ricky Gervais

How was the process of moving out of your college dorm or apartment? How long did it take? How did you feel?

"A good laugh and a long sleep are the two best cures for anything."
– Irish proverb

Have you had the chance to go out and explore your new neighborhood and city? What did you discover?
(Even if you have lived in this city before, see what new places you can find!)

"Habits change into character." – Ovid

What has surprised you about post-graduation life so far?

"Actions prove who someone is. Words prove who someone wants to be."
– Kemmy Nola

What has been harder than you expected?

"The difference between winning and losing is most often not quitting."
– Walt Disney

What has been easier than you expected?

"The secret of getting ahead is getting started." – Agatha Christie

Start listing things that you are thankful for and see how many you can list:

- _____
- _____
- _____
- _____
- _____
- _____
- _____
- _____
- _____
- _____
- _____
- _____
- _____
- _____
- _____
- _____
- _____
- _____

"Never let the things you want make you forget the things you have."
– Anonymous

What are some nearby places you are looking forward to exploring or trying out? *(Your list can include anything of interest: restaurants, parks, museums, hiking trails, sports arenas, theatres, neighborhoods, or cultural attractions.)*

"Promise me you'll always remember: You're braver than you believe, and stronger than you seem, and smarter than you think." – Winnie the Pooh

What made you laugh today?

"Never dim anyone else's light so that you can shine. Just shine."
– Unknown

Do you feel that you have supportive personal and professional networks? How have your friends, family, colleagues, and mentors helped you get to where you are today? How can you 'pay it forward' to help others?

Looking to grow your support network? Smile, be open, and be friendly; take the initiative to talk to and introduce yourself to others, and don't be discouraged—it takes time to develop good friendships and connections, but each day brings you one step closer!

What are some ways you can make your new apartment or room feel more like 'home'?

Shop savvy and budget-smart to find deals as you decorate your new place. Try to put out pictures and other items that remind you of those who love and support you. And use this fresh start to spring clean and donate items you no longer use.

What can't you truly live without? Try to think of what you need versus what you want . . .

"Everything in life is easier when you don't concern yourself with what everybody else is doing." – Unknown

If you could go back in time to give advice to your high school self, what would you say?

"Do your thing. Do it unapologetically. Don't be discouraged by criticism. You probably already know what they're going to say. Pay no mind to the fear of failure. It's far more valuable than success. Take ownership, take chances, and have fun. And no matter what, don't ever stop doing your thing." – Asher Roth

What is your favorite thing so far about your new home?

"What screws us up most in life is the picture in our head of how it's supposed to be." – Unknown

Something that made me smile today:

___

Something nice I did to brighten someone else's day today:

___

"One of the happiest moments in life is when you find the courage to let go of what you can't change." – Unknown

Do you ever struggle to 'be yourself' when meeting new people? When do you find it hardest to be yourself?

"The reason we struggle with insecurity is because we compare our behind-the-scenes with everyone else's highlight reel." – Steve Furtick

Have you been able to find new friends with whom you share common interests? What has been the best way you have found to meet people? What are other things you could try? *(See a list of suggestions on the next page.)*

Looking for places to meet people? Try out a few of these:

- ✓ Walking/running/hiking groups
- ✓ Biking groups
- ✓ Church/temple/mosque/religious groups
- ✓ Local political parties or civic-minded causes you care about
- ✓ Dog parks (meet other pet owners!)
- ✓ Sports leagues (e.g. kickball, dodgeball, volleyball)
- ✓ The local sports bar that supports your favorite team
- ✓ Gym/exercise classes (or yoga or rock climbing—get active!)
- ✓ Photography/ceramics/art classes
- ✓ Wine or beer tasting events
- ✓ Community groups (e.g. Junior League or Rotary Club)
- ✓ Have friends/family introduce you to their friends in the area
- ✓ Improv or acting classes
- ✓ Cooking classes
- ✓ Language classes
- ✓ Volunteering
- ✓ Toastmasters
- ✓ Alumni events
- ✓ Lessons (tennis, golf, archery—what do you want to learn?)

"You cannot change the people around you, but you can change the people you choose to be around." – Unknown

What is something new you have tried in the last month?

"You only live once but if you do it right, once is enough." – Mae West

Is there something you should be doing right now that you are avoiding? What are you waiting for?

"If it's still in your mind, it is worth taking the risk." – Paulo Coelho

How have you been keeping in touch with friends from school? Have you kept in touch with the people you expected to?

"You can easily judge the character of a man by how he treats those who can do nothing for him." – Malcolm S. Forbes

What don't you like about your life right now? What can you do to change this?

"It has been my philosophy of life that difficulties vanish when faced boldly." – Isaac Asimov

How do you like to relax? Have you been doing a good job keeping your stress levels down?

Ways to relax:

-Listen to music

-Get lost in a good book

-Exercise

-Journal

-Hang out with friends

-Laugh

-Cook

-Take slow, deep breaths

-Yoga/stretch

-Meditation

-Get some fresh air

-Dance

-Play a game or do a crossword puzzle

-Play with your pet (or borrow a friend's)

-Plan your next trip

-Light some candles

-Sip chamomile tea

"Remember, today is the tomorrow you worried about yesterday."
– Dale Carnegie

Who or what do you miss the most?

"Isn't it funny how day by day nothing changes, but when you look back everything is different...." – Unknown

What are you excited about?

"Courage doesn't always roar. Sometimes courage is the quiet voice at the end of the day saying 'I will try again tomorrow.' " – Mary Anne Radmacher

What are you curious about?

"You can't control other people. You can only control your reactions to them." – Unknown

What is something new you learned this week?

"If you ever find yourself in the wrong story, leave." – Mo Willems

How do you budget your spending and saving?

___

What mid- and long-term goals are you saving for?

Personal Finance and Budgeting Tips

- Put together a budget (Not sure how? Find a good template online or look up an app that will help)

- Spend less than you make

- Start saving for retirement. If your employer has a 401k, be sure to contribute at least enough to get the company to match it

- Make a list of what you are saving for and look at it often—it's good to remind yourself what you are working toward

- Don't carry a balance on your credit cards

- If you have student loans, make the minimum payment and then seek to pay off the one with the highest interest rate

- Protect yourself: get renter's insurance and health insurance

- Know your credit score

- Save 3 months of living expenses in case of emergency

- Pay your bills on time

- Pay attention to fees and keep them to a minimum (bank fees, ATM fees, credit card fees, expense ratios in your investments)

- Aim to spend 25% or less of your before-tax income on housing

- Pack your lunch, and make your coffee/tea at home or work

- Track your net worth and continue to increase it

- Diversify your investments. Take a personal finance course or do some research to learn more about how to take care of yourself

"You are free to choose, but you are not free to alter the consequences of your decisions." – Ezra Taft Benson

What are you relieved about?

"My entire life can be described in one sentence: it didn't go as planned, and that's ok." – Rachel Wolchin

What are you hopeful about?

"Every time I thought I was being rejected from something good, I was actually being re-directed to something better." – Steve Maraboli

What are your top 5 dream travel spots?

"I'm not sure what I'll do but—well, I want to go places and see people. I want my mind to grow. I want to live where things happen on a big scale."
– F. Scott Fitzgerald

In what ways have you taken advantage of your new, fresh start?

"Life always offers you a second chance. It's called tomorrow."
– Unknown

What have you learned about yourself in the last year?

"Sometimes what we learn and who we become in the process of waiting is even more important than what we're waiting for." – Unknown

What goals do you have for the next 12 months?

_____

_____

_____

_____

_____

_____

_____

Lay out your immediate 'next steps' to start working toward those goals:

_____

_____

_____

_____

_____

_____

_____

_____

_____

"Sometimes what we learn and who we become in the process of waiting is even more important than what we're waiting for." – Unknown

What advice would you give to others who are about to graduate from college?

"The harder you work, the luckier you get." – Gary Player

Notes/Thoughts:

Notes/Thoughts:

> "Go into the world and do well. But more importantly, go into the world and do good."
>
> *— Minor Myers*

AND SO YOUR ADVENTURE BEGINS . . . .

Other products available from Essential Engagement Services:

The Essential Moving Guide: Practical advice to quickly create a sense of belonging and settle in

The Essential Moving Guided Journal: Feel Settled, Sooner

The Essential Moving Guide For Families: Practical advice to ease your family's transition and create a sense of belonging

The Essential Moving Guided Journal (For Teens): My Life and My Thoughts Before and After Moving

facebook.com/EssentialMovingGuide

twitter.com/MyEsntlGuide

pinterest.com/EssentialGuide/